DINO RECORD BREAKERS

THE BIGGEST, FASTEST AND DEADLIEST DINOS EVER!

DARREN NAISH

CARLTON KiDS

CONTENTS

EDMONTONIA

FACT FILE

WHEN:	Cretaceous 70-65 mya
SIZE:	20 ft. (6 m) long
DIET:	Herbivorous
DANGER:	MEDIUM

DINOSAUR FACT FILE

The spikiest dinosaur of all time is Edmontonia (ed-mon-toe-nee-ah). Spikes stuck out sideways from its body, but the long, pointy spines on its shoulders and neck were most amazing of all.

SHORT AND SPIKY

Edmontonia had a wide body. Its back was flat and its legs were short and muscly. It would have been very difficult for predators, such as a T rex, to push it over in a fight.

CHARGE!

Edmontonia's longest spikes curved forward. This dinosaur might have charged when faced by a predator, just like bulls and rhinos do today.

Armor plates to protect neck

Bony lumps around eyes

Sharp-edged spikes

TROODON

FACT FILE

WHEN:	Cretaceous 70-65 mya
SIZE:	8 ft. (2.5 m) long
DIET:	Omnivorous
DANGER:	MEDIUM

BRAINIEST DINOSAUR

Troodon (troo-uh-don) was the "brainiest dinosaur." Its brain was about as big as a tangerine! That might sound quite small, but it's big for a dinosaur.

BRAIN POWER

Animals with bigger brains are better at communicating and remembering. For its body size, Troodon had the biggest brain of any dinosaur.

Biggest eyes for head size

Brain at back of skull

SUPER SENSES

Most of Troodon's brain power was used for seeing and hearing. This helped to make it a very successful hunter.

Feathered body

FACT FILE

WHEN:	Jurassic
	165-155 mya
SIZE:	16 in. (40 cm) long
DIET:	Carnivorous
DANGER:	NONE

MRS "-'S
PREDATOR

MINI HUNTER

People used to think that Anchiornis was a type of ancient bird, but it's really a birdlike dinosaur. It probably hunted lizards and insects.

Anchiornis (an-kee-orr-nis) holds the record for being the smallest known predatory dinosaur. It was only as big as a pigeon!

DINKY DRAGON

Another tiny predator is Mei long, which was about the size of a duck. Its fossil was found curled up, and its name means "soundly sleeping dragon."

Sharp teeth

Three clawed fingers

Long feathers

FACT FIL[E]

WHEN: Cretaceous 125–120 mya

SIZE: 10 ft. (3 m) long

DIET: Herbivorous

DANGER: NONE

LONGEST TAIL

The record for the longest tail compared to the size of its body belongs to Leaellynasaura (lee-ally-nah-saw-rah). Its tail had over 70 bones and was more than three times longer than its head, neck, and body put together.

SCARF TAIL

Leaellynasaura might have wrapped its super-long tail around itself to keep warm, just like snow leopards do today.

LONGEST TAIL EVER!

The longest dinosaur tail ever belonged to Amphicoelias fragillimus. It may have been as long as three buses!

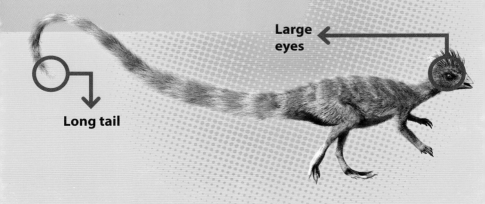

Large eyes

Long tail

HYPSELOSAURUS

FACT FILE

WHEN:	Cretaceous 70–65 mya
SIZE:	49 ft. (15 m) long
DIET:	Herbivorous
DANGER:	MEDIUM

LARGEST EGG

The largest dinosaur eggs found so far are the giant ball-shaped eggs of Hypselosaurus (hip-sell-oh-saw-rus). The largest ones were as big as 73 chicken eggs put together!

COVER UP

Dinosaurs like Hypselosaurus didn't build nests. Instead, they laid their eggs in lines or circles. Then they probably hid the eggs under sand or soil.

Large body ←

Claws for scraping soil or sand over eggs →

EGG RECORD BREAKER

Hypselosaurus laid the biggest dinosaur eggs, but the biggest eggs ever came from a bird named Aepyornis. Nicknamed the "elephant bird," its egg was four times bigger than Hypselosaurus's!

FACT FILE

WHEN: Cretaceous 70-65 mya
SIZE: 13 ft. (4 m) long
DIET: Omnivorous
DANGER: Low

FAST RUNNER

Super speedy dinosaur Struthiomimus (strooth-ee-oh-mime-us) could probably run at about 50 mph (80 kph). That's nearly as fast as a racehorse!

LAND SPEED RECORD

Here's how modern-day fast-running land animals compare with Struthiomimus.

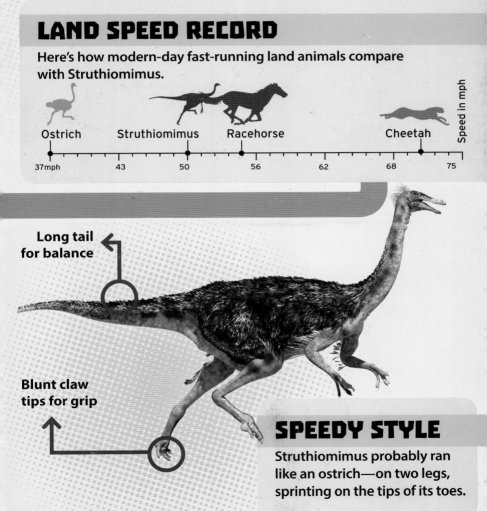

Speed in mph

Ostrich	Struthiomimus	Racehorse		Cheetah	
37mph	43	50	56	62	68	75

Long tail for balance

Blunt claw tips for grip

SPEEDY STYLE

Struthiomimus probably ran like an ostrich—on two legs, sprinting on the tips of its toes.

BIGGEST HEAD

FACT FILE

WHEN:	Cretaceous 75-71 mya
SIZE:	23 ft. (7 m) long
DIET:	Herbivorous
DANGER:	LOW

PENTACERATOPS

Pentaceratops (pen-ta-serra-tops) probably had the biggest head of any land animal that ever lived. Including its enormous frill, this plant-eater's awesome head was as long as a small car.

BIG HEAD

Why did Pentaceratops have such a big head? Some people think that the size and shape of the frill helped to collect sound and made the dinosaur's hearing better.

COOL DUDE

Elephants flap their enormous ears to cool down. Some horned dinosaurs may have used their huge frills to get rid of heat too.

Bony lumps

Skin stretched over skull bones

LIOPLEURODON

ACT FILE

WHEN:	Jurassic 165-145 mya
SIZE:	49 ft. (15 m) long
DIET:	Fish, squid
DANGER:	HIGH

SCARIEST SEA PREDATOR

Liopleurodon (lye-oh-pluur-oh-don) was a plesiosaur. Bite marks found on fossil bones show that it attacked and ate other huge sea reptiles. Some experts think its bite was ten times stronger than a Tyrannosaurus rex's!

DEADLY AMBUSH

Liopleurodon might have grabbed paddling dinosaurs and pulled them into deep water. Killer whales hunt this way today, snatching sea lion pups from the water's edge.

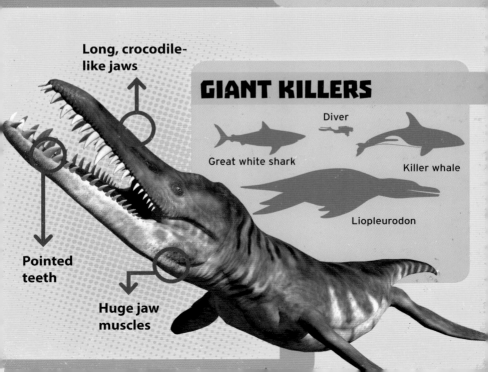

Long, crocodile-like jaws

Pointed teeth

Huge jaw muscles

GIANT KILLERS

Diver

Great white shark

Killer whale

Liopleurodon

BIGGEST
FLYING ANIMAL

FACT FILE

WHEN:	Cretaceous 70-65 mya
SIZE:	36 ft. (11 m) wingspan
DIET:	Omnivorous
DANGER:	HIGH

QUETZALCOATLUS

Gigantic pterosaur, Quetzalcoatlus (ket-zel-kwat-lus) holds the record for being the biggest flying animal ever. Its wingspan was about the same as a World War II Spitfire airplane!

SUPER SOARER

Quetzalcoatlus's wings were shaped like the wings of modern storks and vultures. These birds soar great distances when hunting—Quetzalcoatlus probably did too.

Long neck ←

Strong wing muscles ←

Sturdy wing bones

GROUNDED

Quetzalcoatlus could fold its wings to walk and run on all fours! On the ground, it was similar in size to a giraffe.

AN· I·-., FEATHERS

FACT FILE

WHEN:	Cretaceous 125-120 mya
SIZE:	2 ft. (70 cm) long
DIET:	Carnivorous
DANGER:	NONE

MIC· O· ·TO

The fanciest feathers of all belonged to a tiny dinosaur named "Microraptor" (my-crow-rap-tor). It had a crested head, long arm feathers, and fan-shaped tail feathers. It even had feathers sprouting out of its legs.

FEATHER FINGERS

Microraptor's feathers grew off the fingers as well as the arm bones, just like they do in birds today.

TWIN WING

The long leg and foot feathers of Microraptors are special. Nothing like them exists today. The leg feathers might have given extra lift—just like the extra wing on a biplane.

Fan-shaped tail

Super long leg feathers

Long arm and hand feathers

BIGGEST CLAWS

FACT FILE

WHEN:	Cretaceous 70-65 mya
SIZE:	33 ft. (10 m) long
DIET:	Omnivorous
DANGER:	MEDIUM

Therizinosaurus (thair-ee-zine-uh-saw-rus) was one of the weirdest-looking dinosaurs ever. It had a long neck, a big round belly and record-breaking claws—which may have been up to 3 ft. (1 m) long!

SUPER SLASHER

Therizinosaurus had three claws on each hand. The claws were long, slender, and gently curved, like a saber sword.

Beak

Long neck

Narrow curved claws

KILLER CLAWS

Therizinosaurus was a plant-eater, so why did it have such massive claws? Perhaps it used them to hook branches to eat. Or maybe it used them to defend itself from predators.

TOUGHEST ARMOR

FACT FILE

WHEN: Cretaceous
70–65 mya

SIZE: 23 ft. (7 m) long

DIET: Herbivorous

DANGER: MEDIUM

Armored dinosaurs like Ankylosaurus (an-ky-low-saw-rus) were like dinosaur tanks. Their bodies bristled with armor plates, spikes and horns. Ankylosaurus probably used its heavy tail club to whack predators!

BIG AS A BUS

Ankylosaurus was as heavy as a bus and nearly as long, with a wide, round body. It was almost impossible to tip over!

BULLET PROOF

Ankylosaurus's armor was thin, but very strong—as strong as Kevlar, the material used to make bullet-proof vests!

Bite-proof armor plating

Triangular horns

Club-like tail

FASTEST TAIL

FACT FILE

WHEN:	Jurassic 150-147 mya
SIZE:	105 ft. (32 m) long
DIET:	Herbivorous
DANGER:	HIGH

DIPLODOCUS

Diplodocus (dip-lo-doe-cus) had an amazing tail! Some scientists think its tail was actually used like a whip, and that the tip could be swished at superfast speeds.

WHIP CRACK

Some experts think that the tail-tip of Diplodocus could have been used to make a loud 'crack' to scare other dinosaurs away or to attract a mate.

GENTLE GIANT?

Diplodocus is usually imagined as a "gentle giant," but big modern plant-eaters such as rhinoceroses can be dangerous too. Maybe Diplodocus wasn't so gentle after all!

Skinny tail tip

Tall triangle-shaped spines

Massive tail muscles

PTERANODON

FACT FILE

WHEN: Cretaceous 144-137 mya

SIZE: 8 ft. (2.5 m) long

DIET: Omnivorous

DANGER: LOW

TOOTHIEST PREDATOR

Record-breaking predator Pelecanimimus (pel-e-can-ee-mime-us) had about 220 teeth! That's over three times more than most meat-eating dinosaurs.

GONE FISHING

The jaws of Pelecanimimus were long and shallow. Animals with jaws like this often feed by reaching into water and grabbing slippery prey.

PELICAN PRETENDER

Floppy folds of skin hung down from Pelecanimimus's jaw, like a pelican's pouch. This is where its name, meaning "pelican mimic," comes from.

Tiny closely-spaced teeth

Front teeth for grabbing

Back teeth for slicing

STEGOSAURUS

FACT FILE

WHEN:	Jurassic
	155-145 mya
SIZE:	22 ft. (7 m) long
DIET:	Herbivorous
DANGER:	MEDIUM

BIGGEST SHOW-OFF

HOT STUFF?

Stegosaurus might have used its plates to control its body temperature. They could have soaked up the sun's heat to keep the dinosaur warm, or given off heat to cool down it down.

Enormous diamond-shaped plates grew from the neck, back, and tail of Stegosaurus (steg-oh-saw-rus). These plates were probably used for "showing off" and could even have been brightly coloured.

PLATE PUZZLE

Stegosaurus's plates weren't just made of bone—they also had a horny covering on top. This covering has not survived in fossils, so we don't know how big or what shape it was!

Larger plates on back

Smaller plates on neck

NYCTOSAURUS

FACT FILE

WHEN:	Cretaceous 85-84 mya
SIZE:	7 ft. (2 m) wingspan
DIET:	Fish
DANGER:	NONE

LONGEST HEAD CREST

Pterosaurs were flying reptiles that often had crested heads. The longest crest of all belonged to a pterosaur named Nyctosaurus (nik-tow-saw-rus) that soared over the seas.

SKIN SAILS?

Scientists wanted to see if the crests worked like sails, so they made models of pterosaur heads with crests covered in skin. Their tests showed that skin-covered crests did not work as sails.

WINGING IT

Nyctosaurus's wingspan was similar to that of a Bald Eagle. Its crest was almost as long as one of its wings!

Unusual Y-shape

Crest made of bone

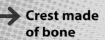

SIZING IT UP!

BIGGEST PREDATOR

FACT FILE

WHEN:	Cretaceous 112–95 mya
SIZE:	59 ft. (18 m) long
DIET:	Carnivorous
DANGER:	HIGH

Spinosaurus (spine-oh-saw-rus) may have been the biggest two-legged predator that ever lived! It was almost twice as long as a bus and weighed more than two elephants.

FISH SUPPER

The narrow snout and jaws of Spinosaurus look similar to those of a crocodile. It probably reached into water to grab fish, rather than killing other dinosaurs on land.

TOP 5 KILLERS

These are the five biggest hunting dinosaurs found so far.
1 ➡ Spinosaurus
2 Giganotosaurus
3 Tyrannosaurus Rex
4 Carcharodontosaurus
5 Mapusaurus

Huge sail on back

Strong, muscly arms

Big claws

FRUITADENS

SELECT A PLANT-EATER

FACT FILE

WHEN:	Jurassic 150 mya
SIZE:	2 ft. (70 cm) long
DIET:	Herbivorous
DANGER:	LOW

The smallest plant-eater discovered so far is little Fruitadens (froot-ah-dens). A fully-grown adult was only about the size of a cat!

SMALL AND SPEEDY

Lots of other dinos would have wanted to eat Fruitadens. Its long tail may have helped it balance so it could run quickly.

DINKY DINOS?

Birds evolved from small dinosaurs, so you could say that tiny dinosaurs are still alive today! This Cuban bee hummingbird is just 2 in. (5 cm) long.

Small fangs

Long, bendy tail

Claws for grabbing

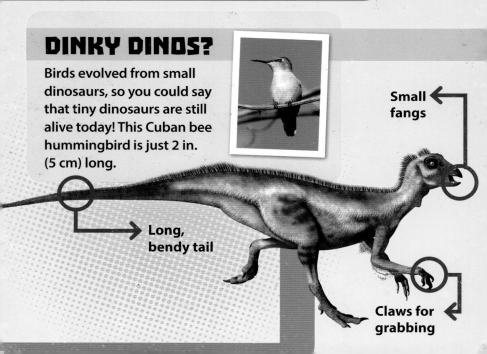

OLDEST BIRD

FACT FILE

WHEN: Jurassic
155-150 mya

SIZE: 20 in. (50 cm) long

DIET: Carnivorous

DANGER: NONE

C   E   TE   YX

The oldest bird we know of is Archaeopteryx (ar-kee-op-ter-rix). Fossils show us that birds evolved from small predatory dinosaurs!

EARLY BIRD

Archaeopteryx would have looked very different from modern birds. It had long clawed fingers and tiny teeth. It probably looked more like a small Velociraptor!

THE SURVIVORS

Birds were the only type of dinosaur to survive the mass extinction that happened 65 million years ago. They probably survived because they were small and could fly long distances.

Long arm feathers

Long tail feathers

Small teeth

TY REX

Sti II Su...ng II IIS

STRONGEST BITE

Tyrannosaurus rex (tie-ran-oh-sore-us rex) wasn't just huge—it also had one of the strongest bites ever. Its bite was six times stronger than an alligator's. It could even bite right through the bodies of its prey!

GIANT JAWS

A Triceratops fossil from Montana had one of its horns bitten clean off by a T rex, while an Edmontosaurus, also from Montana, had a giant T rex bite in its tail. Ouch!

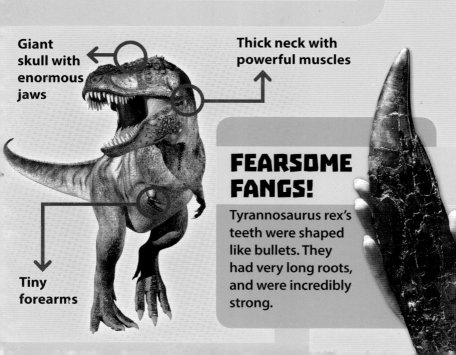

Giant skull with enormous jaws

Thick neck with powerful muscles

Tiny forearms

FEARSOME FANGS!

Tyrannosaurus rex's teeth were shaped like bullets. They had very long roots, and were incredibly strong.

WEIRDEST NECK

FACT FILE

WHEN:	Cretaceous 130-125 mya
SIZE:	43 ft. (13 m) long
DIET:	Herbivorous
DANGER:	MEDIUM

A huge dinosaur named Amargasaurus (ah-marg-ah-saw-rus) had long, bony spines poking out from its neck. These rows of spikes might have even been joined together with skin to make two sail shapes.

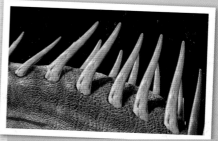

STRANGE SPINES

Armargasaurus had nine pairs of spines growing out of its neck bones. The spines were very long with rounded ends.

PRICKLY PRONGS

Amargasaurus might have used its spines to defend itself from predators, like a porcupine does today!

Bony spines ←

→ Strong neck

PACHYCEPHALOSAURUS

FACT FILE

WHEN:	Cretaceous 70-65 mya
SIZE:	16 ft. (5 m) long
DIET:	Omnivorous
DANGER:	LOW

HARDEST HEAD

Pachycephalosaurus (pack-ee-seff-al-o-saw-rus) had a thick dome like a bowling ball on top of its head. The top of its skull was more than 40 times thicker than yours!

SHOW OFF?

Some experts think that Pachycephalosaurus's bumpy head may have helped it show off to other dinosaurs.

Spiky bumps

Thick skull

Strong legs

TOUGH NUTS

Another idea is that these dinosaurs fought by smashing their heads together, or butting each other like football players!

SAUROPOSEIDON

TALLEST EVER

FACT FILE

WHEN: Cretaceous 115-105 mya
SIZE: 89 ft. (27 m) long
DIET: Herbivorous
DANGER: HIGH

Sauroposeidon (saw-row-pa-side-un) is the tallest dinosaur ever discovered. It was so tall it could have looked into the windows of a six-story building!

HEAVY STEPS

The name Sauroposeidon means "earthquake god lizard". It weighed as much as 10 male African elephants and probably made the ground shake when it walked!

GIANT GUESS

Only a few neck bones of this dinosaur have been found—and some giant footprints—so we don't know for sure if Sauroposeidon was very tall or very long.

Super-long neck

Light neck bones

FUZZIEST DINOSAUR

FACT FILE

WHEN:	Cretaceous 115-105 mya
SIZE:	3 ft. (1 m) long
DIET:	Herbivorous
DANGER:	LOW

One type of dinosaur named Psittacosaurus (sitt-ack-uh-saw-rus) had long, fuzzy, feathery quills that stuck up from its tail. Experts are still trying to work out what the quills were for.

HIDEAWAY

Some modern creatures such as sea dragons use soft, feathery parts of their bodies to help them hide among plants. Perhaps Psittacosaurus used its quills in the same way.

QUILL QUESTION

Psittacosaurus is one of the best known dinosaurs because hundreds of its fossils have been found—but so far only one has been found with tail quills!

Parrot-like
head

Fuzzy
tail quills

LONGEST SPIKES

FACT FILE

WHEN:	Jurassic 164-160 mya
SIZE:	20 ft. (6 m) long
DIET:	Herbivorous
DANGER:	MEDIUM

The longest spikes ever grown by any animal sprouted from the tail of Loricatosaurus (lor-ee-cart-oh-saw-rus). They were probably used to fight off enemies.

ON POINT

Loricatosaurus might have swung its tail spikes from side to side to pierce an attacker's flesh. An Allosaurus tailbone was found with a hole made by a tail spike—probably a stegosaur's.

SLOW WALKER

Loricatosaurus had stubby legs and small feet—and was built for walking slowly. It would have needed the spikes on its tail and spikes to defend itself because it wouldn't have been able to run away from danger.

Shoulder spike

Back plates

Long tail spikes

MOST TEETH

FACT FILE

WHEN:	Cretaceous 65-61 mya
SIZE:	30 ft (9 m) long
DIET:	Herbivorous
DANGER:	LOW

EDMONTOSAURUS

Edmontosaurus (ed-mon-toe-saw-rus) had more than 1,000 diamond-shaped teeth, which makes it the toothiest dinosaur ever! New teeth replaced the old ones as they wore down.

GRINDING JAWS

Edmontosaurus used its teeth for shredding plants. It had a special hinge in the bones of its face that meant it could move part of its skull from side to side to grind down leaves and twigs.

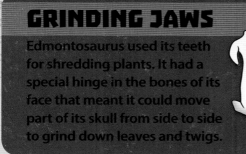

BITING BEAK

We know quite a lot about the beak of Edmontosaurus because, in one fossil, it did not rot away as usual! The beak was similar to the beaks of modern turtles and birds.

Wide beak ←

Large eyes ←

LONGEST HORNS

FACT FILE

WHEN:	Cretaceous 72-70 mya
SIZE:	23 ft (7 m) long
DIET:	Herbivorous
DANGER:	MEDIUM

FRILLY FACE

Coahuilaceratops belongs to the same group of dinosaurs as Triceratops. Most had short nose horns, long brow horns, and a big frill at the back of their head.

Coahuilaceratops (coh-whe-lah-serra-tops) had two huge horns. Each brow horn was nearly as long as a broom handle! This dinosaur must have looked scary, but it ate plants, not other dinosaurs.

HEAD TO HEAD

Horned dinosaurs probably used their horns as weapons to fight among themselves, as well as to fight off predators.

Huge brow horn

Bony lumps on frill

Small nose horn

ULTIMATE
KILLING
MACHINE

FACT FILE

WHEN:	Cretaceous 115-87 mya
SIZE:	23 ft. (7 m) long
DIET:	Carnivorous
DANGER:	HIGH

Utahraptor (yoo-tah-rap-tor) was a ferocious dinosaur with a jawful of terrifying teeth and giant curved claws on its feet and hands. These fearsome weapons made it the ultimate killing machine!

KICKING CLAW

The second toe of each foot had a huge and very sharp curved claw. Utahraptor probably grabbed its prey with its hand claws and then kicked with its curved claw, slicing into flesh!

SLASH AND GRAB

Utahraptor could not turn its wrists. Its hands were fixed, like they were clapping. They would have been used for grabbing small animals or for slashing larger dinosaurs.

Sharp teeth

Curved claws

Short, muscly legs

INDEX

PICTURE CREDITS

The publishers would like to thank the following sources for their kind permission to reproduce the pictures in this book.

Key: t = top, b = bottom, l = left, r = right, c = centre & bk = background

Getty Images: 19 t Sylvain Cordier/Imagebank; /43 br Louie Psihoyos/Science Faction

Istockphoto: 11 t, 39 c, 57 t

Jay Mitchell: 49 c

Photodisc: 29 t

Science Photo Library: 9 b Julius T Csotonyi

Shutterstock: 4 bk, 5 t, 5 c, 6 bk, 8 bk, 9 t, 10 bk, 12 bk, 13 t, 14 bk, 16 bk, 17 t, 17 c, 18 bk, 20 bk, 21 t, 22 bk, 23 t, 23 c, 24 bk, 25 t, 26 bk, 27 t, 28 bk, 29 c, 30 bk, 31 c, 32 bk, 33 c, 34 bk, 35 c, 36 bk, 37 t, 38 bk, 40 bk, 42 bk, 44 bk, 45 c, 46 bk, 47 b, 48 bk, 50 bk, 51 c, 52 bk, 54 bk, 55 c, 56 bk, 58 bk

Every effort has been made to acknowledge correctly and contact the source and/or copyright holder of each picture and Carlton Publishing Group apologises for any unintentional errors or omissions, which will be corrected in future editions of this book.

THIS IS A CARLTON BOOK

© Carlton Books Limited 2018

Editor: Joff Brown
Design Manager: Emily Clarke
Design: Wild Pixel
Production: Nicola Davey

Published in 2018 by Carlton Books Limited
An imprint of the Carlton Publishing Group
20 Mortimer Street, London W1T 3JW, UK

ISBN 978 1 78312 458 9

Printed in China